Glendalough Calling

Poems and Thoughts
inspired by
Glendalough and The Wicklow Hills

By Martin Swords

Glendalough Calling

Poems and Thoughts
inspired by
Glendalough and The Wicklow Hills

This Collection First Published in 2017
This Edition Published in February 2024
Copyright © Martin Swords 2017

All rights reserved. This book may not be reproduced in whole or in part by any process without written permission from the copyright holder.

Published by Martin Swords
swords.martin@gmail.com

ISBN: 978 1544622552

Cover Image: The Upper Lake
Frank Corry Glendalough PhotoPost

*Dedicated to the memory of
Darren Brack (1982 - 2014)
Our Godson, who died far too young at 32.
We held a 'Walk for Darren' in Glendalough
during his treatment.*

Glendalough

Glendalough is a magnificent scenic valley in the heart of the Wicklow Mountains.
The valley was glacially formed in the last Ice Age period in Ireland, about 20,000 years ago. It is one of a series of seven parallel valleys in the Wicklow Mountains, all similarly formed. Glendalough – from the Gaelic - Gleann Dá Loch – The Valley of the Two Lakes - is the most spectacular and scenic of all and probably the richest in term of History, Folklore and Story. All of these valleys are isolated and difficult to reach, but well worth the effort, especially Glendalough.
It was the very isolation of this valley that was attractive to Saint Kevin, an early Celtic Christian Hermit, born approx 500 A.D. He chose to live a hard life there, to pray and meditate in this harsh environment, making a prayer of his difficult life of isolation. Fame of his holiness and of Glendalough as a holy place, soon spread and attracted followers and students, perhaps to Kevin's annoyance. After the death of Kevin around 600 A.D. followers kept coming to this 'Holy' place.
Over the next 600 years Glendalough grew into a major centre of Monasticism and Pilgrimage, far outgrowing the small community founded by Kevin at the upper Lake, requiring the development of a much larger community and Monastic Centre lower down the valley – the present Monastic City. This famous Monastic Site, a university-like centre of learning and devotion, became the pre-eminent centre of pilgrimage and study in an era

when Ireland was known as 'The Island of Saints and Scholars.'

Glendalough was famous throughout Ireland, the Continent and further afield, with a surprising amount of travel and studious exchange between Ireland, and ancient centres of study in the Middle East, following the sacking and destruction of old knowledge treasuries and libraries. Monks from Glendalough and other Irish Monastic Sites, in their efforts to establish new monasteries in Europe, are credited with 'Bringing the Light of Learning back into the Europe of The Dark Ages' – described by some as a saving of civilization. The Golden Era of Glendalough was probably in the period 750 A.D through 1250 A.D.

During this period of Monastic fame and fortune, the site of Glendalough was attacked often, both from The Vikings who raided from their newly formed stronghold of the City of Dublin, and by the local clans or 'septs', extended families who lived in wild and difficult mountainous terrain. In Wicklow the local septs were mainly The O'Byrnes, The Kavanaghs, and the O'Tooles. These local septs attacked the Viking stronghold of Dublin, and trading sites like Dalkey, Bray and Wicklow. Among the reasons for attacking Monastic sites like Glendalough were gold and silver money, treasures, jewels and precious stones used in religious artefacts such as reliquaries; food, the monasteries were largely self sufficient, a main food source in Glendalough being huge herds of pigs foraging in the valley, and the monks ate rather well, influenced by their own sense of 'special holy importance', privilege, and the deference shown to clergy by their faithful followers, while the attacking septs were starving in the wilds of the Wicklow Mountains; and last not least attacks were to capture 'slaves' during these raids. Captured slaves were taken away in chains to work, or more likely to be sold quickly to traders or pirates, where they might end up in North Africa or the Middle East, perhaps even as far away as Russia, to work out their lives and never set eyes again on 'Beautiful Glendalough'.

The decline of Glendalough followed the Norman Invasion and a changing political and religious-freedom climate over the next 800 years, in a radically changing Ireland.

Yet right up to modern times, in a twentieth and twenty-first century Independent Ireland, Glendalough continues to be loved, respected, and valued for its magical mystical atmosphere, offering modern pilgrimage, eco-spirituality, a sense of renewal and re-discovery of self, - and like the monks of old, the beneficial and life affirming effects of living in the heart of nature.

I gave guided walks in Glendalough enabling others to learn more of its history, folklore and legends in my Guided 'Walking Talks', helping visitors to discover and love Glendalough – as I do.

Martin Swords
Glendalough Guided Walks

Contents

Calling	11
Glendalough Speaks Quietly	12
I Am Wicklow	13
Lazy Beds	14
Listen	15
A Winner in Wicklow	16
As I Came Over Wicklow Gap	17
A Tree Has Fallen	18
Blackbird	20
Bullaun Stone Magic	21
Carols	23
A View from Tiglin	25
A Walk in the Woods with Robert Frost	26
Sharp Night in Glendalough	28
Far from Athy	30
Glendalough - The Valley of the Two Lakes	31

Contents continued

Glendalough Suite	33
Green Girl	35
Lights in the Valley	36
Listening at Sally Gap	38
Mountain Stream Song	40
Hermitage	41
Plastic Daffodils	43
Saint Kevin's Cross at Glendalough	44
The Garden at Tiglin	46
Walk a Different Road	47
Wicklow Lighthouse 3 a.m.	49
Zen in the Country	50
The Golden Water	51
About the Author	53

During the course of my Guided Walks I met a wide variety of people, groups and nationalities. On one occasion I well remember I was guiding a party of Native American guests from New York State. One of them said to me – 'This place is calling, this place speaks to me, to people like me who can hear'. The phrase stayed with me, hence the title of this collection. I hope you hear Glendalough calling to you too.

Martin

Calling

something
draws me
to this place
quiet
peace
the sound of water
spilling over stone
empty echoes
wind in winter
lapping lakespit
rain
dripping down
sedges softly
is it a need
a call
being answered

Martin Swords

Glendalough Speaks Quietly

Glendalough speaks quietly to me
It speaks of peace, tranquillity, patience
It speaks of pilgrims past and pilgrim ways
It speaks renewal, discovery of self
Of nature's gifts and eco-spirituality

Glendalough tells old tales
Of Saints and Scholars
Of hard lives lived as prayers
Of Dark Ages and The Light of Learning
Illuminating a Continent

Glendalough whispers fear of persecution
Mass paths and Mass rocks in the hills
Secret signs for that which was forbidden
Of old ways hidden in the heart
Of a downtrodden people

Glendalough speaks with new urgency
In changing threatening times
Old values, old customs, healing wells,
Cloothies hanging on a faery tree
Old ways still speak of nature,
Telling us a magic mystic lesson for today

Martin Swords December 19th 2016. Read at The Christmas Carol Service in The Cathedral Ruins in The Monastic City, Glendalough.

I Am Wicklow

I am a Big River and a Small River
I am a Valley of Two Lakes
I am a Norse Name, a Grassy Meadow
I am a Toothless Monk
I am a Stag on a Boggy Hill
I am a Glen where a Devil Lives
I am a Seal at a Fishman's Shop
I am a Mackerel with a Bright Eye
I am a Red Kite with No Strings
I am Brown Bread marked with a Cross
I am a Garden for All Seasons
I am an Old Place with Young Blood
I am the Gorse on a Stony Field
I am a Stubborn Sheep
I am a Safe Harbour in a Storm
I am the Shifting Stones on a Wave Washed Shore
I am a Market Town where Little is Sold
I am a Hungry Child unable to Eat the Scenery.

Martin Swords
October 2016

Lazy Beds

Lazy Beds are areas where potatoes were grown, often in times of hardship.They were an urgent solution, poor farming opportunities where needs were great. They are a series of raised ridges formed by turning sods and earth from right and left to form the raised ridges in which potatoes were planted and grown. Lazy Beds were often used on sloping hillsides and poor quality ground, they were very effective. Long after the people, the potatoes, and the need were gone, the ridges remain visible on the land throughout Ireland, a testimony to hard times past.

Lazy was not the word for it
Hardwon. Backbreaking.
Little enough return for effort
Lumpers. Poor nourishment. Fear and Famine.

Ridged soil scratched on unlikely hills
Where hope grew better than food
Overgrassed abandoned now
Sower and Harvester gone to grow in Newfoundland.

You did not seek to make a monument
Only a meal, or a grave
Yet your Lazy Beds have left a message
Your unintended story written in the ground.

Martin Swords

Listen

Walking Up The Green Road

In Glendalough

'Listen', she said

'I hear nothing' I replied.

'That's it', she said

'You do hear it

I thought it was just me'

'Lovely, isn't it', she said later.

Martin Swords

A Winner in Wicklow

Dropping in
To the newspaper shop
In Roundwood,
Easy, familiar.
'The Irish Times,
A packet of Classic cigars,
Milk, a dozen farm eggs,
And the Radio Times if it's in.'
The shop fills with noisy
Talk and greetings,
Weather and wisdom,
Words and wit.
Justine smiles.
Bridie glows.
Warm ways.
Warm welcomes.
'Oh, and three lines of Lotto with no plus.'
What else is worth winning?
Money?

Martin Swords
31st May 2005

As I Came Over Wicklow Gap

In Ireland we call a pass over the mountains - a 'Gap' - this one has spectacular scenery and follows the Pilgrim Path from Hollywood - to Glendalough.

As I came over Wicklow Gap
All on a summer's day
A sight I met which held me trapped
And took my breath away
A view emerged as if to say
Stop and remember well today
Treasure the memory from this day
Before you're on your way, now
Before you're on your way

As I came over Wicklow Gap
All in a summer still
The sun shone on the mountain cap
A single shaft of golden spill
And lit ablaze the very hill
I can recall it still
If ever my spirit's ill
It lifts my heart and always will, now
I know it always will

Martin Swords
May 2009

A Tree Has Fallen

i.m. Tommy Nolan 1940 - 2008

In a silent belfry
An old bell.

From the sea at Wicklow
A new rope.
In the graveyard
A new sound.
The Tolling Bell
Calls loud
To the quiet hush
Of the slow walk.
Ask not for whom,
It tolls for Tommy Nolan.

Back from the valley
Forest hills,
Derrybawn,
Lugduff, Camaderry,
Brockagh,
The toll returns,
The woodland wakes
A sturdy forester.
A tree has fallen,
Back to the earth.
Ring on Toll.
Echo Thanks.

Martin Swords   August 2020

A Poem.

And thanks for the Life and Work of Seamus Heaney.

Blackbird

i.m. Seamus Heaney 1939 - 2013

The Blackbird is no more
In sweet Glanmore
And yet still
The songs he sang
Sing on and echo
Rebounding and redoubling
Far beyond the Wicklow Hills
Mossbawn to Moscow
Navan, Nullarbor
In Athens, Ashford and Athy
The song is heard
Trilling, growing, soaring.
Listen.
Listen well.

Martin Swords
September 2013

Bullaun Stone Magic

How many strikes of stone
striking iron striking rock
did it take to make you
How many years of grinding
did it take to shape you
How many potions
cures and blessed balms
were mixed in your vessel cup
How many pilgrims paid for
your real or crooked cures
their slim hopes, their prayers,
their aspirations hanging
on your bullaun blessing,
your stone age magic

Without their belief you were
only a hole in a stone

Martin Swords
November 2009

Bullaun Stones are stones, usually granite, with a basin-like shape carved into them. 'Bullaun' is a gaelic word meaning vessel, cup, or basin, the stones are manmade, and are widely found at Monastic sites and in particular Glendalough in County Wicklow. They are a development from the earlier Quern Stone, and like a pestle and mortar were used for grinding herbs or materials for metalwork, preparation of paint or ink for manuscripts. It is also believed that at Monastic Pilgrim sites they were used to make medicinal, herbal and perhaps Blessed potions to sell to willing and receptive pilgrims. In Glendalough the most famous Bullaun Stone is The Deer Stone associated with one of the legends of Saint Kevin.

Carols

Silent Night in Glenealy Church.
Serried voices sang unpolished this moving
Heartfelt echo from the trenches, for that first
Choir of youth, dead names on brass plaques

St. Kevin's Church in Glendalough,
A cold church and a warm congregation.
Late on a dark frosty Eve, signs of Peace,
Handshakes and Well Wishes.

Angela and the choir, *Adeste*.
Catherine on the high notes, *Gloria*.
O Holy Night sung to rapt quiet
Listening, tear filled eyes and sniffles

A child Virgin, a child Joseph,
A Jesus for the Crib.
Young children at Church, keen
Anticipation on sleepy faces.

Bethlehem,
The Western Front.
Glenealy.
Laragh,
Glendalough.

Silent Nights.
Memories of Carols.
Memories of Christmas Eves.
This is Christmas.

All the rest is only shopping.

St. Stephen's Day
26 December 2009

This poem recalls attendance at Christmas Carol Services in Ballymoate Church of Ireland, Glenealy and St Kevin's Catholic Church, Laragh. A number of brass plates in Ballymoate Church in Glenealy commemorate the loss of local officers and men in WW1.

A View from Tiglin

I sat once
in the garden in Tiglin
as sunset slipped
behind the hill at Moneystown
into the holy well of Glendalough
A silver plane, a pod
of people, golden jet
trail caught in crimson,
chasing the westward sun,
blazed across the blue.

Who are you people
bound for Boston,
Newark or beyond.
Are you happy going,
going home or going on.
Or is your journey sad,
to say goodbye, to
scatter memories on
a Staten Island sea.
Half a couple, broken.
Rushing onwards
too high, too fast, to see.
You'll never know the beauty
of the picture you were part of,
beyond Moneystown,
looking from the garden
in Tiglin.

Martin Swords   June 2004

A Walk in The Woods with Robert Frost

Overcast but warm,
The day dry, unusually.
Walking the woods with the dogs
As many times before.
Lucy and Tiggy, away in the rough dark deepwood,
Yipping with the scent of deer, excited.
Ruby, river scrambling, biting
At the bogwater, wagging her tail,
From the shoulders back

Along the old familiar track into
The clearing where the roads diverge.
I stopped and stood. Which way to go?
Think of another Poet, and roads not taken.
Yes, I've been here before. This way I came.
That way I saw a squirrel once.
And down that way a badger.
Straight on, the Mill Pond where ducks dabble.
Behind me then a stag, stares my way, and
Startled, slips into the wood.

I think again of Robert Frost and look a different way.
I stand a while. I turn, retrace my steps, recall, relive,
I know, I'll write this down, and this will be
The road I've taken.

Martin Swords
June 2007

Sharp Night in Glendalough

night air in Glendalough is sharp,
sharp frost is on the ground
the frozen puddles hold
the Dog Star shining down
the Green Road sparkles icy
cold stillyness the sound
from Derrybawn as streamlets
stand in icicles hung down

on Paddock Hill the ring of stones
four thousand years stood round
hoarfrost stubbles granite face
facing Camaderry's mound
firm footprints of the furtive
deer trail shadows on the ground
breath clouds in the still night air
as each hilly step is bound

in homes of long gone foresters
windows flicker winter warmth
valley folk in their cosy cots
sit ruddy faced at fiery hearths
in this the place they love,

this mountain Glen
this magic mystic Glendalough
alive in the sharp night air

Martin Swords
February 2008

Far from Athy

Pat told stories of old times, living in digs
in Athy, working on the roofin' for aul' Hammond.
Me with my booklearning piped up
"I heard of Athy,
"And look! a barge comes bringing from Athy
And other far-flung towns, mythologies." ",
lines from the canalbankpoet.*
"Bet he never saw it in the lashing
rain", Pat observed dryly.
No. Nor I had never seen it Pat's way,
from a cold slate roof breaking galvanised
tacking nails with the long ripper,
and only the price of two pints in his pocket,
till Friday.

He was glad for me that I hadn't.

Martin Swords   May 2009

i.m. Pat Swords 1915 - 1978
On His Birthday 1st May

*From Lines Written On A Seat On The Grand Canal, Dublin,
"Erected To The Memory Of Mrs. Dermot O'Brien"*

By Patrick Kavanagh

Glendalough - The Valley of the Two Lakes

Thousands of visitors come to Glendalough every year. Many are in a rush to see, to photograph and go on. They don't get to see Glendalough as it really is, quiet, peaceful and good for the spirit.

Walk slowly,
In slowly slanting sun
Down the Valley of the Two Lakes

Listen,
At rocks edge, ripples
Like a cat lapping

Watch,
As lazy heron casts
A fishy eye

All is quiet
All is still
In the Valley of the Two Lakes.

Around the Tower, dizzy
Clicks and whirring
Picture everything
Picture the peace
Click the calm
Shout about the quiet
Record. Replay. Forget.
Move on and never know

The sweet nothing
That is everything
In the Valley of the Two Lakes.

The Hermits knew
When they found it,
That nothing

But the Hand of God
Quietly touched
The Valley of the Two Lakes

Martin Swords   May 2020

Glendalough Suite

Derrybawn
*Hill of the white oak grove,
beloved of Nelson's fleet.
Victory left the valley folk burning faggots.*

Lugduff & Poulaneass
*Black Hole Mountain Brook,
father of the two lakes.
Powerful force,
a torrent in streams clothing.
Speaks to us in splashes now
of the ice that spawned it.*

Spink
*Master view of lakes and valley,
Treacherous pointed rock.
luring unwary travellers
to a sloping edge too far*

Tonlegee
*Tón Le Gaoithe, 'Back To the Wind'.
Always the wind, from every direction.
Many an Ice Age since you were warm.
many the bitter blast a Phóg Do Thón.*

Camaderry
The Pass of the Oak Wood,
nobly named in ages past
before the rape for ships and mineshafts

Brockagh
Once a village,
 proud, hardwon, hardmade.
Now even Broc himself
finds life hard on this bare and barren rock

Glendalough
Magic mystic valley
cradled in its mountain arms
even in winter, warmly welcoming

Martin Swords   January 2012

Green Girl

I guided a group of teenagers from the City of Dublin. One girl in a green jacket, a true 'Dub', a real hard ticket, a city girl, was determined not to like the countryside, but she did really, grudgingly, she was open to Wonder. I hope she recalls it well2

Feisty and smart on the outside
Her soul shone through sparkling eyes.
Green Girl. Child of nature.
Without admitting,
She loved The Valley of Two lakes.
Green jacketed
She fitted into the story.
Only in Glendalough a little
But a little of Glendalough
Will live in her forever.
She will recall.

Martin Swords
Glendalough Guided Walk
October 20th 2014

Lights in the Valley

Listen.
Listen to the lights.
Speaking silently, steadily.
Calling us, out of the dark.
There were always lights in the valley.
The lights of learning,
The illuminating lights of scribes,
Beacons in The Dark Ages.
The safe lights for the hard road
Underground, on days bright or black.
Now, in changing times
There is a new light in the valley.
The light of community,
The light called "Together",
The light of transition
From a time of wasted plenty,
To depending on each other.
Keep this new light burning,
Shelter and nurture it to see the future.
Listen to the light speaking.
Little lights, held high by children,
Showing us much more
Than just the stony path ahead.

Martin Swords   October 2010

Theme poem for the 'Lights in the Valley'
Glendalough Arts Network
Community Event
Children's Lantern Walk
Glendalough Valley
22 October 2010

Listening at Sally Gap

*Sally Gap is a mountain pass, or Gap, high in the Wicklow Mountains.
It has nothing at all to do with a woman's name, there is no 'Sally',
though I often hear tourists refer to the name as 'Sally's Gap'.
In fact the place is named after the Sallie or Willow bushes which grew
there. This is the same sense used in the famous Irish song 'Down by the
Sally Gardens'.
That is 'the gap of the way or road of the sallies/ willow bushes'.
Sailearnán possibly means 'a place of willows'.*

There is always a wind
one or other of the four winds blowing
moaning with the loneliness of the place
soft ground tough grass and hard sheep.

Ghosts of silent footed rebels tramping to the
safety of their mountain valley holds
before the Military.
The wind still carries their shouts

their cries their pleadings and their hopes
mixing with the bleak empty sounds of this place
a trickle of water on stone
a gurgle of water on wet black turf

Is that the thin echo of a sleán slicing sods,
or that heavy hollow sound, the turf-cutter's
clunkin' bottle of sweet milky tea
corked with a scruntch of newspaper

Or a bit of broken fence banging in the wind

Martin Swords   May 2009

Mountain Stream Song

As a silver comb slips
through newborn golden hair,
soft stream trickles
merrily through the moss.

With plith and splinkle
the drops play
their mountain music
on the organ stones

I stop and listen
sharing the nascent song,
enchanted,
soaring,
searching for the words

© *Martin Swords   January 2007*

Hermitage

Many's the fainthearted
Full of fear and fright
Guided from dark danger
By the calling bell and light

Some are the downtrodden
Seeking to find their way
Some are the lost forgotten
Journeying out to pray

Others seek the hallowed ground
To stand where Kevin stood
To walk by the lake where Kevin walked
To the Saint's cell in the wood

Most are good God fearing
Knowing right from wrong
Longing to touch the hermits hem
To grow in the hermits song

Longing to touch the hermits hem
To rest in the sanctuary found
To grow in the way of the hermits step
In Glendalough Holy ground

To grow in the way of the hermits step
To find in themselves again
The simple truth of quiet content
The core of self, the inner being
The honest look, that way of seeing
The hermits gift, the hermits tranquil way

Martin Swords   October 2009

Plastic Daffodils

I wandered lonely as a prayer
Along the monks path by the Glendasan
When all at once around a rocky bend
I saw a sight afloat to make me take a stand
A host of plastic bottles thrown away
Waving their caps and labels o'er the land
I often think in solitude so grand,
For all their cheap and handy ways
Discarded plastic bottles of today
Are simply just too big a price to pay
And then my heart with sorrow fills
A refuse sack with plastic bottle daffodils

Martin Swords   February 2009

With apologies to William Wordsworth

Saint Kevin's Cross at Glendalough

Solid squat stubborn
Your granite face stands silent
Well your Monastic Masons carved
Your message of the old and new
Together, the Cross of new Salvation
The Sun Circle of the old
Old and New in one

This hard granite page
bore a subtle soft message
as if written on calf skin Vellum
by a goose given quill
in dark berry blood
written softly in a Saintly hand
The Celtic Cross
The message of was
And is, and will be
Together

Martin Swords   April 2016

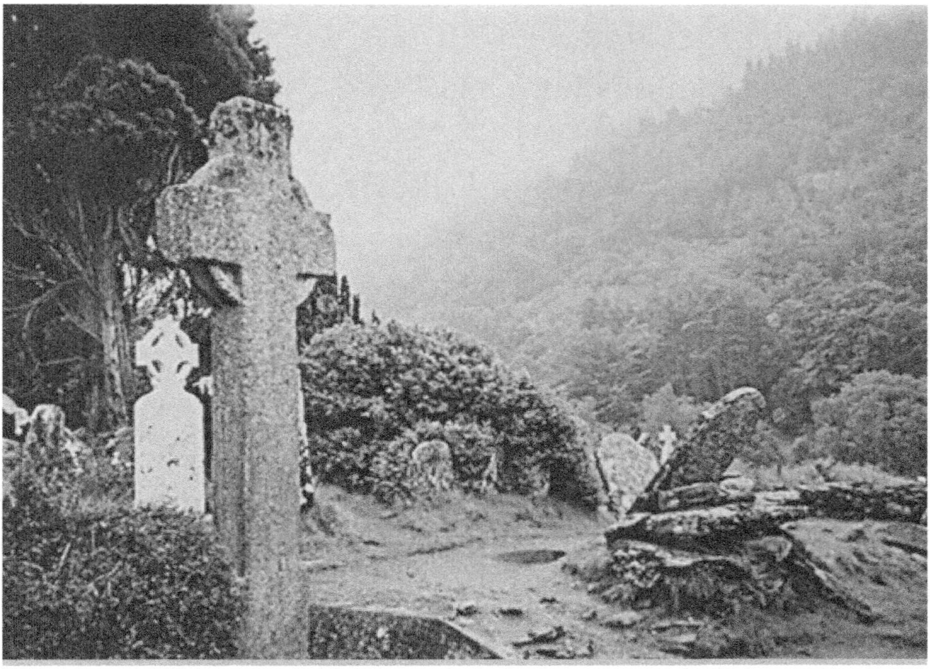

The Garden at Tiglin

This is David and Fiona's Cherry tree
A gift of ripe rich red
This is Mark and Naomi's tall Red Oak
Everreaching.
This is Jacinta's Wedding Cake Tree
Slowly growing into its shape.
This Robinia is Sean's Tree
It once was small and frail
Now it is big and beautiful
This is Martin's Orchard
Three Cookers for the table
This is the garden at Tiglin
Not perfect, but just like us.

Martin Swords
May 2011

Walk a Different Road

December 21st Winter Solstice 2015. Carol Service in the Cathedral Ruins. The Monastic City, Glendalough.

We are at the turning of the year
Here in Gleann Dá Loch
This Spiritual site, this font of nature
As we celebrate Juul, Solstice Fire, Christmas,
Darkness into Light, the Turning of the Year
Here let us remember the Ancients,
 Ancient Ways, early Celtic Christian Monks
And Caoimhinn* who spoke to the fishes, birds and trees
Let us return to live with nature and value it
Repair the damage we have done on the road we travelled
'I cannot save the world by myself, but I can play my part
Be aware, consume, waste and destroy less,
feed the birds and bees, grow more, plant a tree, plant a forest'
Maybe we cannot speak to nature as Caoimhinn* did
But we can listen; we must listen as it says –
'Enough, change your ways,
See the light and turn to
Walk a different road'

Martin Swords   December 2015

Wicklow Lighthouse 3a.m.

The form of this poem's opening and closing sections is based on the BBC's famous 'Shipping Forecast', read twice daily on BBC Radio 4, and listened to by many thousands, in the UK and Internationally - including me listening in County Wicklow in Ireland.

"... A deepening depression... heavy rain...
... poor visibility ... strong southerly winds
...veering southwest
... building strong gale after midnight... "

Shine, steady light,
and bring them home
to Wicklow

Dear God, look out for Jim
and all the lads aboard the Sarah Ann,
struggling home against the wind
beyond the Arklow Sands

Shine steady, light,
and bring them home
to Wicklow

And all for what? Less
fish than ever, every time,
a box of crabs, a living?
A hundred hooks, a life, all on the line.

Shine strong now, light,
shine strong all night
and bring them home
to Wicklow

Your daughter Sarah, soon, I hope
will have a brother.
And they will need their Father
then, to love them, and their Mother.

Shine steady strong and surely
show their way
and bring them home
to Wicklow, safe, today.

"... reports are coming in... fishing vessel... no contact
... sighted... approaching Wicklow harbour ...
                         ...just after 3a.m. ..."

Martin Swords   16 November 2005

Zen in the Country

All in green
Many shades
Yet all is green
in Glendalough

The golden leaves
Are not dying
They are transmuting
Into life

A day comes
When you sense it
A change of air
Autumn

Martin Swords
January 2014

The Golden Water

The Golden Water
Of a Wicklow Mountain stream
Is it Gold? No.
Is it Silver? No.
It's the liquid sunshine of the bog
Carried in golden streams away
The everturning process of Life,
Decay and Transformation

Old ground of silky silt
Looking for a new home
Swept From Aughavannagh
To Arklow's shore
From Knockananna
To Kilcool shingle

I see it in Glendalough
In Tiglin and Annamoe
A fleeting glimpse of golden
Rushing over rocks

Through sedge grass sieves
I marvel at the colour,
The journey, and the wonder of it all

Martin Swords   December 2014

People often ask me why the Wicklow Mountain streams are a brownish colour, it's not dirt, it's sunshine really, from the bog.

End papers for the 2017 Edition

About the Author

Martin Swords is a member of Wicklow Writers Group.

He ran Glendalough Guided Walks, giving Walks 'n Talks in the Monastic City and The Valley of Glendalough.

He has a background in Communications, Radio and Graphic Design. He has been writing Poetry and short stories since 1990.

Martin is published in "Lifelines New and Collected", "Voyages", Wicklow Writers Anthology, "A View from Tiglin", "The Space Inside", Wicklow Arts Magazine, "Anniversary" Anthology celebrating Ten Years of Wicklow Writers; The Prairie Schooner Ireland Edition Winter 2011, University of Nebraska U.S.A., New York Times Blog, and various editions Glendalough and Laragh News.

You can also hear him read three of his poems on 'Voices from the Shore', a CD of poems and stories by Wicklow Writers, and on "Kathleen's Child", Glendalough Arts Network Website. You will also find his work and performances on You Tube under 'Martin Swords Channel'.

Martin has performed at many venues over the years, including Tinahely Arts Courthouse Café, Kilruddery House, Wicklow Library, The Brockagh Gallery Glendalough, the Space Inside Arts Club Wicklow and at The Fireside Sessions by the Glendalough Arts Network, The Patriot Inn, Kilmainham, and Whelan's Live Downstairs, Wexford Street, Dublin.
He lives in Tiglin, Co. Wicklow

Thank You

Martin Swords

Links

http://glendaloughguidedwalks.com/
http://wicklowwriters.blogspot.com/
http://martinswordspoetry.wordpress.com/
swords.martin@gmail.com

Watch Martin's video, 'Kathleen's Child', for more information about Martin.
It is on You Tube under Martin Swords Channel

Martin

End papers for the 2024 Edition

Other books by Martin Swords

Five by Five by Five / 2012

A Letter to Mary / 2016

Glendalough Calling / 2017

The Last Little Wood / 2017

Story? / 2018

Ramblings on my Mind / 2020

Tea in the Burlington - A Memoir / 2021

STREET - 19 Findlater Street Stories / 2023

https://www.amazon